PAQUITO D'RIVERA

LA FLEUR DE CAYENNE

(Venezuelan Joropo)

for Flute and Piano

HENDON MUSIC

BOOSEY & HAWKES

DISTRIBUTED BY

7777 W. BLUEMOUND RD. P.O. BOX 13819 MILWAUKEE, WI 53213

www.boosey.com
www.halleonard.com

This work is also available for the following instrumentations:

Clarinet in B♭ and Piano
Oboe and Piano
Soprano Saxophone and Piano
Trumpet in C
Violin and Piano
Clarinet in B♭, Violoncello, and Piano
Flute, Bassoon, and Piano
Clarinet in B♭, Tenor Saxophone (or Bassoon), and Piano
Clarinet in B♭, Bass Clarinet, Violoncello, and Piano
String Quintet
Clarinet in B♭ and String Quintet

LA FLEUR DE CAYENNE

Venezuelan Joropo

PAQUITO D'RIVERA

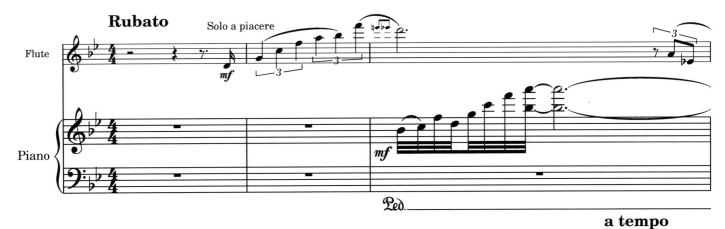

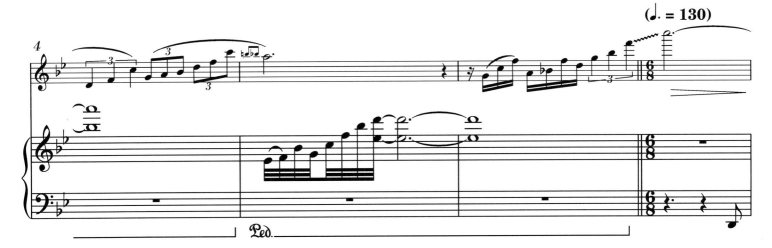

Performance Note: All indicated articulations are suggested, and may be altered at the discretion of the performer.

979-0-051-09822-4

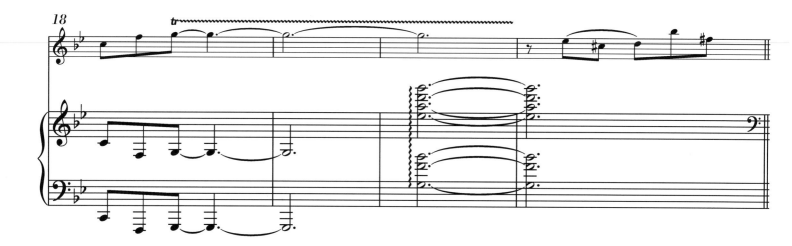

A Tempo Joropo

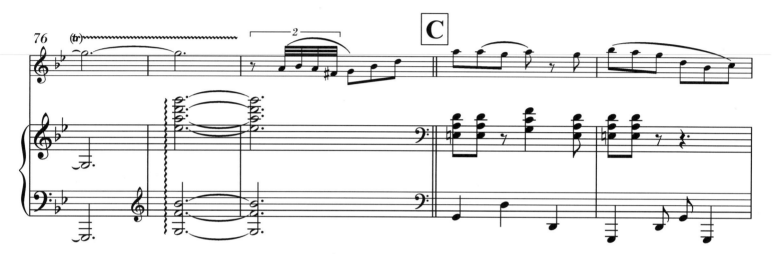

PAQUITO D'RIVERA
LA FLEUR DE CAYENNE

(Venezuelan Joropo)

for Flute and Piano

HENDON MUSIC

DISTRIBUTED BY

7777 W. BLUEMOUND RD. P.O. BOX 13819 MILWAUKEE, WI 53213

www.boosey.com
www.halleonard.com

Flute

LA FLEUR DE CAYENNE
Venezuelan Joropo

PAQUITO D'RIVERA

Performance Note: All indicated articulations are suggested, and may be altered at the discretion of the performer.

979-0-051-09822-4

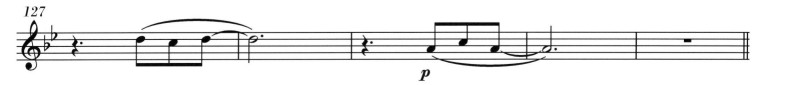

Salsa Feel ♩. = ♩ (♩ = 130)

Tempo Primo

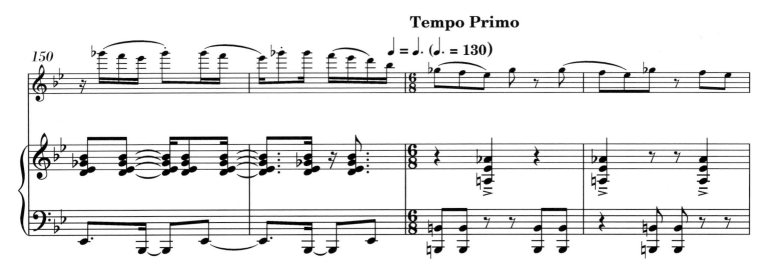

F